LIFE CYCLES

The Butterfly

Diana Noonan

CHELSEA CLUBHOUSE

An Imprint of Chelsea House Publishers
A Haights Cross Communications Company
Philadelphia

Chelsea Clubhouse
1974 Sproul Road, Suite 400
Broomall, PA 19008-0914

The Chelsea House world wide web address is www.chelseahouse.com

Library of Congress Cataloging-in-Publication Data

Noonan, Diana.
    The butterfly / by Diana Noonan.
    p. cm. — (Life cycles)
    Summary: An introduction to the physical characteristics, behavior, and life cycle of
    the insect that changes from an egg to a caterpillar to a butterfly.
    ISBN 0-7910-6963-X
    1. Butterflies—Life cycles—Juvenile literature. [1. Butterflies.] I. Title. II. Series.
    QL544.2 .N66 2003
    595.78'9—dc21

                                                                        2002000028

First published in 1999 by
MACMILLAN EDUCATION AUSTRALIA PTY LTD
627 Chapel Street, South Yarra, Australia, 3141

Copyright © Diana Noonan 1999
Copyright in photographs © individual photographers as credited

Edited by Anne McKenna
Text design by Polar Design
Cover design by Linda Forss

Printed in China

Acknowledgements

Cover: The wanderer (monarch) butterfly collecting pollen from a sunflower. (Auscape © Densey Clyne)

A.N.T. Photo Library, pp. 4 © Silvestris, 5 © J. Frazier, 8, 26 © Frithfoto, 11 & 30 © B.G. Thomson, 17 & 30, 24 & 30 K.K. Vagg, 18 © J. Kiely, 19, 25 © F. Mercay, 22 © K. Uhlenhut, 23 © I.R. McCann, 27 © F. Park, 28 © C. Webster, 29 & 30 © N.H.P.A.; Auscape, pp. 6, 7 © Jean-Paul Ferrero, 9, 10 © Pascal Goetgheluck, 12, 13, 20, 30 © A. & J. Six, 14 © J. Shaw, 15, 16 © K. Atkinson, 21 © C.A. Henley.

While every care has been taken to trace and acknowledge copyright, the publisher tenders their apologies for any accidental infringement where copyright has proved untraceable.

Contents

Life Cycles

All animals change as they live and grow. They begin life as tiny creatures. They grow into adults that will produce their own young. The butterfly has its own special life cycle.

Butterflies Are Insects

Butterflies are insects. An insect has a head, a **thorax**, and an **abdomen**. It has a pair of **antennae** that help it smell and feel. An insect also has six legs and either two or four wings.

Butterflies have four wings. Tiny colored scales cover each wing.

Like all insects, butterflies are cold-blooded animals. Their bodies are as warm or as cold as the air around them.

These butterflies are migrating for the winter.

Butterflies live all over the world except in the very hottest and very coldest places. In winter some butterflies hibernate. They go into a deep sleep. Others **migrate** long distances to warmer places.

Protection

Other insects and birds eat butterflies. The colors and patterns on a butterfly's wings are **camouflage**. The camouflage helps the butterfly blend into its surroundings and hide from **predators**.

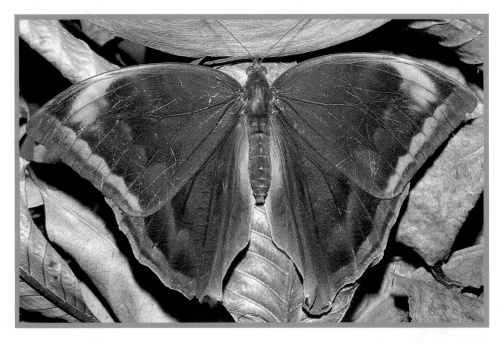

A butterfly hides among dead leaves.

eye-spots

Some butterflies are bright colors. The colors warn predators that these butterflies are poisonous to eat. Some butterflies have eye-spots on their wings. A bird may think that the butterfly is a large animal with big eyes.

Courting

A butterfly **courts** when it is ready to **mate**. It shows off its bright colors to attract a partner.

These butterflies are trying to attract a partner.

Mating

The male and female butterflies join together at their tail ends to mate. Some butterflies fly as they mate.

A pair of butterflies mate.

Laying Eggs

Soon after mating, the female butterfly is ready to lay eggs. She flies to a plant that she knows her young will want to eat.

This butterfly is laying her eggs on a cabbage leaf.

The eggs stick to the leaf.

She uses a sticky substance from her body to attach her eggs to the plant. The sticky substance protects the eggs from heat and cold. It keeps them from drying out.

Inside the Eggs

Caterpillars grow inside the butterfly's eggs. The eggs turn darker as the caterpillars grow larger.

A butterfly egg holds a caterpillar.

The eggs turn dark as the caterpillars grow.

In spring and summer, a butterfly's eggs may take only two or three weeks to hatch. In autumn and winter, the weather is cooler. The eggs may not hatch for several months.

From Egg to Caterpillar

The caterpillar chews its way out of the egg and begins to eat. Caterpillars often eat many times their weight in green plants in one day. They grow quickly.

A caterpillar hatches from an egg.

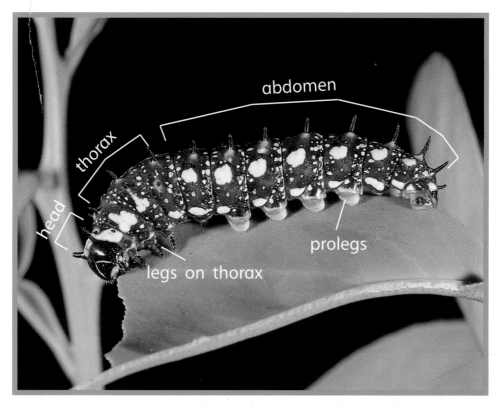

abdomen

thorax

head

legs on thorax

prolegs

The caterpillar has six legs on its thorax.
It has ten prolegs on its abdomen. The
prolegs have either hooks or suction pads.
The prolegs help the caterpillar crawl and
hold onto plants.

Keeping Safe

Some caterpillars use camouflage to protect themselves. They are the same color and pattern as the plants they live on.

This caterpillar looks like it is part of a leaf.

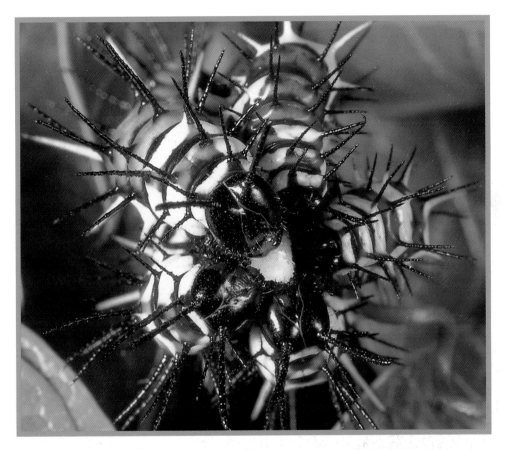

A bird may see these five caterpillars as one animal.

Some young caterpillars stay close together in a clump for protection. A bird sees the clump as one animal that is too big to eat.

Molting

A caterpillar **molts** as it grows. Its skin becomes tight and splits. The caterpillar crawls out of its old skin. It waits for its soft new skin to harden. Then it begins eating again.

A caterpillar sheds its skin when it molts.

old skin

caterpillar

A caterpillar molts four or five times before it
is full grown. It looks for a sheltered place to
rest when it is ready to molt for the last time.

A Resting Place

A caterpillar drops liquid from its body onto a leaf or twig. The liquid turns into a sticky pad. The caterpillar will use the pad to attach itself to its resting place. Some caterpillars make silk threads to hold themselves in place.

silk thread

This caterpillar is resting on a twig.

From Caterpillar to Pupa

The caterpillar's skin splits and falls away.
The caterpillar does not have new skin.
Instead, it has changed into a pupa.

old skin splitting

pupa emerging

This caterpillar is molting for the last time.

The pupa has a case that hardens around the caterpillar. Inside the case, the caterpillar is changing into a butterfly.

This pupa is attached to a twig.

From Pupa to Butterfly

The pupa stage lasts from a few days to several months. The butterfly is then fully formed. It splits open the pupa case. The butterfly's wings are damp and crinkled.

pupa case

crinkled wings

A butterfly breaks out of the pupa case.

The butterfly pumps blood from its body into the **veins** in its wings. The butterfly stretches out its wings until they are flat. Now it is ready to fly.

veins

Metamorphosis

The change from egg to caterpillar to butterfly is called metamorphosis. All insects go through some kind of metamorphosis.

Food for a Butterfly

Some butterflies have jaws and eat plants. Most butterflies have a long **proboscis** to suck **nectar** from flowers. The nectar is food for butterflies.

proboscis

This butterfly is taking nectar from a flower.

Life Span

Butterflies may live for only a day or two.
Some live for a few weeks or a few months.

The Life Cycle of a Butterfly

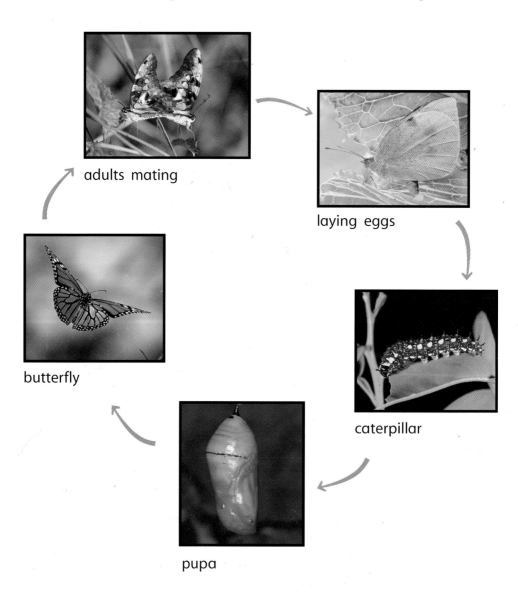

adults mating

laying eggs

caterpillar

pupa

butterfly

Glossary

abdomen   the back section of an insect's body

antennae   long feelers on an insect's head

camouflage   natural coloring that helps an animal hide in its surroundings

court   to try to attract a mate

mate   to join with a breeding partner to produce young

migrate   to travel from one place to another

molt   to shed skin, hair, scales, or feathers and grow a new body covering

nectar   the sweet liquid found in flowers

predator   an animal that hunts other animals for food

proboscis   a long tube that butterflies use to suck nectar from flowers

prolegs   small, leg-like stumps

thorax   the middle section of an insect's body

veins   tiny tubes in the butterfly's wings through which blood flows

Index